I USE MATH/USO LAS MATEMÁTICAS

I USE MATH IN THE KITCHEN/
USO LAS MATEMÁTICAS EN LA COCINA

Joanne Mattern

Reading consultant/Consultora de lectura: Susan Nations, M.Ed., author/literacy coach/consultant

WR WEEKLY READER
EARLY LEARNING LIBRARY

Please visit our web site at: **www.earlyliteracy.cc**
For a free color catalog describing Weekly Reader® Early Learning Library's list of high-quality books, call 1-877-445-5824 (USA) or 1-800-387-3178 (Canada). Weekly Reader® Early Learning Library's fax: (414) 336-0164.

Library of Congress Cataloging-in-Publication Data available upon request from publisher. Fax (414) 336-0157 for the attention of the Publishing Records Department.

ISBN 0-8368-6002-0 (lib. bdg.)
ISBN 0-8368-6009-8 (softcover)

This edition first published in 2006 by
Weekly Reader® Early Learning Library
A Member of the WRC Media Family of Companies
330 West Olive Street, Suite 100
Milwaukee, WI 53212 USA

Managing editor: Valerie J. Weber
Art direction: Tammy West
Cover design and page layout: Dave Kowalski
Photo research: Diane Laska-Swanke
Photographer: Gregg Andersen
Translators: Tatiana Acosta and Guillermo Gutiérrez

Printed in the United States of America

1 2 3 4 5 6 7 8 9 09 08 07 06 05

Note to Educators and Parents

Reading is such an exciting adventure for young children! They are beginning to integrate their oral language skills with written language. To encourage children along the path to early literacy, books must be colorful, engaging, and interesting; they should invite the young reader to explore both the print and the pictures.

I Use Math is a new series designed to help children read about using math in their everyday lives. In each book, young readers will explore a different activity and solve math problems along the way.

Each book is specially designed to support the young reader in the reading process. The familiar topics are appealing to young children and invite them to read and reread again and again. The full-color photographs and enhanced text further support the student during the reading process.

In addition to serving as wonderful picture books in schools, libraries, homes, and other places where children learn to love reading, these books are specifically intended to be read within an instructional guided reading group. This small group setting allows beginning readers to work with a fluent adult model as they make meaning from the text. After children develop fluency with the text and content, the book can be read independently. Children and adults alike will find these books supportive, engaging, and fun!

Nota para los maestros y los padres

¡Leer es una aventura tan emocionante para los niños pequeños! A esta edad están comenzando a integrar su manejo del lenguaje oral con el lenguaje escrito. Para animar a los niños en el camino de la lectura incipiente, los libros deben ser coloridos, estimulantes e interesantes; deben invitar a los jóvenes lectores a explorar la letra impresa y las ilustraciones.

Uso las matemáticas es una nueva colección diseñada para que los niños lean textos sobre el uso de las matemáticas en su vida diaria. En cada libro, los jóvenes lectores explorarán una actividad diferente y resolverán problemas de matemáticas. Cada libro está especialmente diseñado para ayudar a los jóvenes lectores en el proceso de lectura. Los temas familiares llaman la atención de los niños y los invitan a leer y releer una y otra vez. Las fotografías a todo color y el tamaño de la letra ayudan aún más al estudiante en el proceso de lectura.

Además de servir como maravillosos libros ilustrados en escuelas, bibliotecas, hogares y otros lugares donde los niños aprenden a amar la lectura, estos libros han sido especialmente concebidos para ser leídos en un grupo de lectura guiada. Este contexto permite que los lectores incipientes trabajen con un adulto que domina la lectura mientras van determinando el significado del texto. Una vez que los niños dominan el texto y el contenido, el libro puede ser leído de manera independiente. ¡Estos libros les resultarán útiles, estimulantes y divertidos a niños y a adultos por igual!

— Susan Nations, M.Ed., author, literacy coach,
and consultant in literacy development

Let's make cookies! I like chocolate
chip the best!

- - - - - - - - - - - - - - - -

¡Vamos a hacer galletas! ¡Mis favoritas son
las que tienen trocitos de chocolate!

How many people are wearing aprons?

¿Cuántas personas llevan delantal?

5

First, we get out all the ingredients.
We need flour, sugar, eggs, vanilla, salt,
baking soda, and chocolate chips.

- - - - - - - - - - - - - - - -

Primero, sacamos todos los ingredientes.
Necesitamos harina, azúcar, huevos,
vainilla, sal, bicarbonato de soda y
trocitos de chocolate.

How many ingredients do we need?

¿Cuántos ingredientes necesitamos?

We need two cups of flour. There are two half cups in every cup of flour.

Necesitamos dos tazas de harina. En cada taza de harina hay dos medias tazas.

We need half a cup of sugar. I pour it into the bowl.

––––––––––––––––

Necesitamos media taza de azúcar. La echo en el cuenco.

Do we use more flour or more sugar?

¿Usamos más harina o más azúcar?

I give Mom the eggs. She cracks them and plops them into the bowl.

Le doy los huevos a mamá. Ella los rompe y los deja caer en el cuenco.

How many eggs do we need?

¿Cuántos huevos necesitamos?

13

Next, I stir in the vanilla, baking soda, and salt. Don't forget the chocolate chips!

Después, echo y mezclo la vainilla, el bicarbonato de soda y la sal. ¡Y no te olvides de los trocitos de chocolate!

What is the last ingredient that we add?

¿Qué ingrediente es el último que agregamos?

14

Mom turns on the oven. The temperature has to be 375 degrees.

- - - - - - - - - - - - - - - - -

Mamá enciende el horno. Tiene que estar a una temperatura de 375 grados.

Is the temperature greater than 300 degrees or less than 300 degrees?

¿Es la temperatura mayor de 300 grados o menor de 300 grados?

I put the cookies on the cookie sheet.
They have to bake for thirteen minutes.

- - - - - - - - - - - - - - - - -

Pongo las galletas sobre la bandeja.
Tienen que hornearse por trece minutos.

The cookies have been baking for eight minutes.
How many more minutes do they need to bake?

Las galletas se han horneado por ocho minutos.
¿Cuántos minutos más tienen que estar en el horno?

Our cookies are done. They taste great!

- - - - - - - - - - - - - - - -

Nuestras galletas están listas.
¡Están deliciosas!

How many cookies did we make?
Hint: Do not forget to count the cookies we are eating!

¿Cuántas galletas horneamos?
Sugerencia: ¡No te olvides de contar las
que nos estamos comiendo!

Glossary

aprons — clothing that you wear to protect your clothes when you cook

degrees — units for measuring temperature

ingredients — items that something is made from

sheet — a flat metal pan for baking

temperature — how hot or cold something is

Glosario

bandeja — utensilio de metal plano para hornear

delantal — prenda que se usa para proteger la ropa mientras se cocina

grados — unidades para medir la temperatura

ingredientes — cosas con las que se hace algo

temperatura — grado de calor o frío de algo

Answers

Page 4 – 1
Page 6 – 7
Page 8 – 4
Page 10 – flour
Page 12 – 2
Page 14 – chocolate chips
Page 16 – greater
Page 18 – 5
Page 20 – 8

Respuestas

Página 4 – 1
Página 6 – 7
Página 8 – 4
Página 10 – harina
Página 12 – 2
Página 14 – trocitos de chocolate
Página 16 – mayor
Página 18 – 5
Página 20 – 8

22

For More Information/Más información

Books

Keeping Track of Time: Go Fly a Kite! Math Monsters (series). John Burstein (Weekly Reader® Early Learning Library)

Pizza Counting. Christina Dobson (Charlesbridge Publishing)

Libros

El niño cocinero Latinoamerica/The Latin American Cookbook for Children. Patricia Van Rhijn (CIDCLI)

Soy buena para las matemáticas. Eileen M. Day (Heinemann Library)

Websites

Kids Are Cooking
www.kidsrcooking.com
A collection of simple and fun recipes for cooking with children

Index

baking soda 6, 14
chocolate chips   4, 6, 14
cups 8, 10
degrees 16
eggs 6, 12
flour 6, 8, 10
ingredients 6, 14
oven 16
salt 6, 14
sheet 18
sugar 6, 8, 10
temperature 16
vanilla 6, 14

Índice

azúcar 6, 8, 10
bandeja 18
bicarbonato de soda 6, 14
grados 16
harina 6, 8, 10
horno 16
huevos 6, 12
ingredientes 6, 14
sal 6, 14
tazas 8, 10
temperatura 16
trocitos de chocolate 4, 6, 14
vainilla 6, 14

About the Author

Joanne Mattern is the author of more than 130 books for children. Her favorite subjects are animals, history, sports, and biography. Joanne lives in New York State with her husband, three young daughters, and three crazy cats.

Información sobre la autora

Joanne Mattern ha escrito más de 130 libros para niños. Sus temas favoritos son los animales, la historia, los deportes y las biografías. Joanne vive en el estado de Nueva York con su esposo, sus tres hijas pequeñas y tres gatos juguetones.

24